The Essential Buyer's Guide

NORTON
COMMANDO

Your marque

Peter Henshaw

VELOCE PUBLISHING
THE PUBLISHER OF FINE AUTOMOTIVE BOOKS

Alfa Romeo Alfasud (Metcalfe)
Alfa Romeo Alfetta: all saloon/sedan models 1972 to 1984 & coupé models 1974 to 1987 (Metcalfe)
Alfa Romeo Giulia GT Coupé (Booker)
Alfa Romeo Giulia Spider (Booker)
Audi TT (Davies)
Audi TT Mk2 2006 to 2014 (Durnan)
Austin-Healey Big Healeys (Trummel)
BMW Boxer Twins (Henshaw)
BMW E30 3 Series 1981 to 1994 (Hosier)
BMW GS (Henshaw)
BMW X5 (Saunders)
BMW Z3 Roadster (Fishwick)
BMW Z4: E85 Roadster and E86 Coupé including M and Alpina 2003 to 2009 (Smitheram)
BSA 350, 441 & 500 Singles (Henshaw)
BSA 500 & 650 Twins (Henshaw)
BSA Bantam (Henshaw)
Choosing, Using & Maintaining Your Electric Bicycle (Henshaw)
Citroën 2CV (Paxton)
Citroën DS & ID (Heilig)
Cobra Replicas (Ayre)
Corvette C2 Sting Ray 1963-1967 (Falconer)
Datsun 240Z 1969 to 1973 (Newlyn)
DeLorean DMC-12 1981 to 1983 (Williams)
Ducati Bevel Twins (Falloon)
Ducati Desmodue Twins (Falloon)
Ducati Desmoquattro Twins – 851, 888, 916, 996, 998, ST4 1988 to 2004 (Falloon)
Fiat 500 & 600 (Bobbitt)
Ford Capri (Paxton)
Ford Escort Mk1 & Mk2 (Williamson)
Ford Focus RS/ST 1st Generation (Williamson)
Ford Model A – All Models 1927 to 1931 (Buckley)
Ford Model T – All models 1909 to 1927 (Barker)
Ford Mustang – First Generation 1964 to 1973 (Cook)
Ford Mustang – Fifth Generation (2005-2014) (Cook)
Ford RS Cosworth Sierra & Escort (Williamson)
Harley-Davidson Big Twins (Henshaw)
Hillman Imp (Morgan)
Hinckley Triumph triples & fours 750, 900, 955, 1000, 1050, 1200 – 1991-2009 (Henshaw)
Honda CBR FireBlade (Henshaw)
Honda CBR600 Hurricane (Henshaw)
Honda SOHC Fours 1969-1984 (Henshaw)
Jaguar E-Type 3.8 & 4.2 litre (Crespin)
Jaguar E-type V12 5.3 litre (Crespin)
Jaguar Mark 1 & 2 (All models including Daimler 2.5-litre V8) 1955 to 1969 (Thorley)
Jaguar New XK 2005-2014 (Thorley)
Jaguar S-Type – 1999 to 2007 (Thorley)
Jaguar X-Type – 2001 to 2009 (Thorley)
Jaguar XJ-S (Crespin)
Jaguar XJ6, XJ8 & XJR (Thorley)
Jaguar XK 120, 140 & 150 (Thorley)
Jaguar XK8 & XKR (1996-2005) (Thorley)
Jaguar/Daimler XJ 1994-2003 (Crespin)
Jaguar/Daimler XJ40 (Crespin)
Jaguar/Daimler XJ6, XJ12 & Sovereign (Crespin)
Kawasaki Z1 & Z900 (Orritt)
Land Rover Discovery Series 1 (1989-1998) (Taylor)
Land Rover Discovery Series 2 (1998-2004) (Taylor)
Land Rover Series I, II & IIA (Thurman)
Land Rover Series III (Thurman)
Lotus Elan, S1 to Sprint and Plus 2 to Plus 2S 130/5 1962 to 1974 (Vale)
Lotus Europa, S1, S2, Twin-cam & Special 1966 to 1975 (Vale)
Lotus Seven replicas & Caterham 7: 1973-2013 (Hawkins)
Mazda MX-5 Miata (Mk1 1989-97 & Mk2 98-2001) (Crook)
Mazda RX-8 (Parish)
Mercedes-Benz 190: all 190 models (W201 series) 1982 to 1993 (Parish)
Mercedes-Benz 280-560SL & SLC (Bass)

Mercedes-Benz G-Wagen (Greene)
Mercedes-Benz Pagoda 230SL, 250SL & 280SL roadsters & coupés (Bass)
Mercedes-Benz S-Class W126 Series (Zoporowski)
Mercedes-Benz S-Class Second Generation W116 Series (Parish)
Mercedes-Benz SL R129-series 1989 to 2001 (Parish)
Mercedes-Benz SLK (Bass)
Mercedes-Benz W123 (Parish)
Mercedes-Benz W124 – All models 1984-1997 (Zoporowski)
MG Midget & A-H Sprite (Horler)
MG TD, TF & TF1500 (Jones)
MGA 1955-1962 (Crosier)
MGB & MGB GT (Williams)
MGF & MG TF (Hawkins)
Mini (Paxton)
Morgan Plus 4 (Benfield)
Morris Minor & 1000 (Newell)
Moto Guzzi 2-valve big twins (Falloon)
New Mini (Collins)
Norton Commando (Henshaw)
Peugeot 205 GTI (Blackburn)
Piaggio Scooters – all modern two-stroke & four-stroke automatic models 1991 to 2016 (Willis)
Porsche 356 (Johnson)
Porsche 911 (964) (Streather)
Porsche 911 (991) (Streather)
Porsche 911 (993) (Streather)
Porsche 911 (996) (Streather)
Porsche 911 (997) – Model years 2004 to 2009 (Streather)
Porsche 911 (997) – Second generation models 2009 to 2012 (Streather)
Porsche 911 Carrera 3.2 (Streather)
Porsche 911SC (Streather)
Porsche 924 – All models 1976 to 1988 (Hodgkins)
Porsche 928 (Hemmings)
Porsche 930 Turbo & 911 (930) Turbo (Streather)
Porsche 944 (Higgins)
Porsche 981 Boxster & Cayman (Streather)
Porsche 986 Boxster (Streather)
Porsche 987 Boxster and Cayman 1st generation (2005-2009) (Streather)
Porsche 987 Boxster and Cayman 2nd generation (2009-2012) (Streather)
Range Rover – First Generation models 1970 to 1996 (Taylor)
Range Rover – Second Generation 1994-2001 (Taylor)
Range Rover – Third Generation L322 (2002-2012) (Taylor)
Reliant Scimitar GTE (Payne)
Rolls-Royce Silver Shadow & Bentley T-Series (Bobbitt)
Rover 2000, 2200 & 3500 (Marrocco)
Royal Enfield Bullet (Henshaw)
Subaru Impreza (Hobbs)
Sunbeam Alpine (Barker)
Triumph 350 & 500 Twins (Henshaw)
Triumph Bonneville (Henshaw)
Triumph Herald & Vitesse (Ayre)
Triumph Spitfire and GT6 (Ayre)
Triumph Stag (Mort)
Triumph Thunderbird, Trophy & Tiger (Henshaw)
Triumph TR2 & TR3 - All models (including 3A & 3B) 1953 to 1962 (Conners)
Triumph TR4/4A & TR5/250 - All models 1961 to 1968 (Child & Battyll)
Triumph TR6 (Williams)
Triumph TR7 & TR8 (Williams)
Triumph Trident & BSA Rocket III (Rooke)
TVR Chimaera and Griffith (Kitchen)
TVR S-series (Kitchen)
Velocette 350 & 500 Singles 1946 to 1970 (Henshaw)
Vespa Scooters – Classic 2-stroke models 1960-2008 (Paxton)
Volkswagen Bus (Copping)
Volkswagen Transporter T4 (1990-2003) (Copping/Cservenka)
VW Golf GTI (Copping)
VW Beetle (Copping)
Volvo 700/900 Series (Beavis)
Volvo P1800/1800S, E & ES 1961 to 1973 (Murray)

First published in April 2010 by Veloce Publishing Limited, Veloce House, Parkway Farm Business Park, Middle Farm Way, Poundbury, Dorchester, Dorset, DT1 3AR, England. Fax 01305 268864/e-mail info@veloce.co.uk/web www.veloce.co.uk or www.velocebooks.com
Reprinted April 2016 & November 2019. ISBN 978-1-787116-52-8/UPC 6-36847-01652-4

Introduction

– the purpose of this book

The Norton Commando is one of the definitive British postwar twins (a lot of Norton owners would no doubt say it's the best of the bunch). Alone amongst British bikes, it sought to beat the traditional bugbear of vibration with an innovative rubber mounting system that kept those twin-cylinder vibes away from the rider. And it remains a fine A-to-B road bike, good over distance, and (if looked after) capable of delivering lots of reliable, and fun, miles.

The Norton Commando can make a very practical classic.

This book is a straightforward, practical guide to buying one secondhand. It won't list all the correct colour combinations for each year, or delve into the minutae of year-by-year changes (there are excellent books listed at the end of this one which do all of that). Hopefully, though, it will help you avoid buying a lemon.

It's hard to believe now, but the Commando was put into production as a stopgap. When Norton's ambitious plans for an all-new superbike came to nothing,

The high-piped 750S was just one of the variations.

its engineers were ordered to come up with an alternative in just three months. Incredibly, they did, and the Commando was unveiled at the Earls Court Motorcycle Show in October 1967. It caused a sensation – the 750cc twin was a lightly modified version of the old Atlas engine, but the bike's radical 'fastback' styling and the promise of a vibration-free ride impressed just about everyone. It was soon voted Machine of the Year by *MCN* readers, and would do so five years running.

Early road tests seemed to live up to the promise. Here was something as quick as any 750cc superbike – it could sprint to 60mph in just over 5 seconds, and top speed was close to 120mph. And the isolastics really did work, as, once over 2500-3000rpm, the big twin's vibration melted away.

Trouble surfaced with the over-tuned Combat version of the twin, but the Commando continued to sell well, and Norton offered a wide range of variations on the basic theme: Fastback, Roadster, Interstate, and even a Peter Fonda-inspired Hi-Rider. As the 750 became an 850, the Commando's character changed as it gained weight and became more of a tourer, but underneath it was still the same bike. In all, Norton built around 60,000 of them.

Any Commando makes a good choice as a practical classic. It's still a fast, characterful machine that can cover long distances, and Commando specialists offer a whole range of components to make it better than new. Spares backup is excellent, so good, in fact, that Norvil can even build you a brand new Commando.

This book could not have been written without the help of a great many people. So, hats off to Les Emery at Norvil, Nick Hopkins at Andover Norton, and to Mick Hemmings, all of whom were generous with their time. Thanks also go to Norton owners Kevin Charles, and the ever cheerful Neil Shoosmith of the Norton Owners Club. And to Andy Westlake, who kindly donated some pictures. Norvil also supplied some of the pictures, and Nick Hopkins read the text and made useful comments. Without people like this, there would be far fewer Commandos on the road today.

And now you can buy a new one – this is a 2007 Commando.

Contents

The Essential Buyer's Guide™ currency
At the time of publication a BG unit of currency "●" equals approximately
£1.00/US$1.22/Euro 1.11. Please adjust to suit current exchange rates
using Sterling as the base currency.

1 Is it the bike for you?
– marriage guidance

Reasonable running costs, good parts availability.

Tall and short riders
Commando 750s are relatively light by modern standards, but the 850s (especially the MkIIIs) are much heavier. All have tallish seat heights (775-825mm), which isn't good news for the short-legged; you sit on top of the bike rather than 'in' it.

Running costs
Lower than you might think. Fuel consumption is nothing special, at 40-45mpg, but Commandos are not hard on consumables, and spares aren't expensive. *At the time of writing,* all pre-1973 bikes (so none of the 850s) are exempt from road fund duty in the UK.

Maintenance
Make no mistake, any bike from this era needs more TLC and sympathy than a modern machine. You'll need to change the oil every 2000 miles to maximise engine life (preferably using monograde 50, not a modern multi-grade) and just keep an eye open for things coming loose or going out of adjustment. The Commando is definitely not a 'ride it, forget it' sort of bike.

Kickstarting
All except the MkIII 850s are kickstart only, but don't let that put you off – it's more

about technique than strength, and an engine in good condition with electronic ignition will readily kickstart.

Usability
Commandos are not urban commuters. The weight, harsh suspension and low speed vibration makes them awkward to ride in traffic. On the open road, though, in top gear, or on long motorway hauls, they excel. Some riders cover high touring mileages each year.

Parts availability
Excellent. With a few exceptions, every part is available, and one specialist (Norvil) can actually build you a brand new Commando. There are several specialists offering good quality parts, and with parts being made all the time, this should continue.

Parts costs
Parts are reasonably priced, despite the Commando's acquisition of 'classic' status – they generally cost less than equivalent Japanese bike parts.

Insurance group
Go for a classic bike limited mileage policy, such as that offered by Carole Nash or Footman James, and you won't pay much for insurance.

Investment potential
Norton made around 60,000 Commandos, and many of those have survived, on both sides of the Atlantic. All will hold their value, but only a genuine Production Racer has real potential as an investment.

Foibles
The Commando's isolastic system is unique, but needs regular servicing, which is more time consuming on the pre-MkIII bikes. The front mounting, which is exposed to the weather, needs more attention than the rear.

Plus points
A gruff, torquey and relaxed big twin, but smoother than any rival thanks to the isolastics. The know-how is there to make any Commando a good long-distance bike, and practical transport.

Minus points
Needs looking after to keep it up to scratch, and not everyone gets on with kickstarting.

Alternatives
Plenty of British twins to choose from – Triumph, BSA, Royal Enfield, etc – but none of them have the Norton's isolastics. Don't forget the Laverda 750 twin, though.

The Commando spares situation is excellent, with nearly all parts available, including such fundamentals as frames and crankcases. There are several knowledgeable specialists providing a wide range of new parts, and Andover Norton International has new parts made (these are often superior in quality to the originals). The Norton Owners Club also offers parts, both new and secondhand.

Complete restoration (basket case to concours) – around ●x10,000

Air cleaner element ●x15.81
Alternator ●x231
Brake shoes rear ●x36
Brake shoes front ●x30
Brake pads ●x27
Brake disc ●x120
Battery ●x26
Camshaft ●x167
Carburettor slide ●x12
Clutch diaphragm spring ●x36
Clutch cable ●x12.65
Cylinder barrel ●x752

Electronic ignition (Boyer) ●x84
Frame (750) ●x713
Fork stanchion ●x40 each
Fuel tank ●x414
Gasket set ●x35
Gearbox mainshaft ●x111
Headlamp ●x73
Mudguard (front) ●x64
Mudguard (rear) ●x75
Oil pump ●x167
Rear chain ●x49

Pistons (850, pr) ●x196
Primary chain ●x23
Rear shock ●x81
Seat (Interstate) ●x138
Silencer (750 Interstate) ●x92 each
Speedometer ●x90
Tank badge ●x4.5
Valve guides ●x12
Wiring loom (pre-MkIII) ●x50
Complete bikes (price in UK) new from ●x12,529

Top far left: Vernier adjusters for the isolastics are available new, and are retro-fittable.

Bottom far left: Even new cylinder heads are being made.

Left: Upgrades, like twin front discs, aren't cheap, but definitely 'do the business.'

3 Living with a Commando

If you've never owned a classic bike, think hard before buying a Commando.
Modern bikes need only an oil check and chain tweak between major services, but
the Norton demands a lot more TLC than that – it's not a 'ride and forget it' sort
of motorcycle; nor is it suitable for everyday commuting. We live in an age where
mechanical devices keep on working without much attention. Old motorcycles
aren't like that.

So, as with any older bike, the Commando needs keeping an eye on, even
between services. Riders get into a mindset of looking out for loose nuts and
blown bulbs. Is that the beginning of a leak from the rev counter drive? Is the clutch
cable in need of some lube? Of course, some riders would say this is all part of the
attraction – by looking after a bike like this, one develops a relationship with it that is
arguably lacking with a modern machine that never goes wrong and always starts
'on the button'.

Having said that, Commandos were used as everyday bikes when they were
new, though back then, most riders were keen twenty-somethings who accepted
that intensive maintenance was part of motorcycling. And even now, there are
Norton Owners Club members who attend all the European rallies each summer,
and who cover upwards of 20,000 miles a year. This is only possible if you have the
appropriate mindset, and take advantage of modern componentry.

Those high-mileage folk are in the minority, and most surviving Commandos are
used as second or third bikes, tucked away in the garage for most of the time, and
wheeled out on sunny days only. Such bikes might cover only 2000 miles a year.
On the other hand, don't be put off if the bike you are looking at is a high-mileage
one – owners of these machines are usually highly knowledgeable, and lavish a
great deal of care on their bikes. If they're Norton Owners Club members, that's a
good sign, and if they've owned the bike for many years, better still. Incidentally,
the Club offers an excellent booklet, *Commando Service Notes*, written by experts
and crammed with practical experience, hints and tips. Originally published in 1979,
it's just as relevant today. While we're on the subject of printed matter, the Haynes
manual isn't rated very highly, but the original factory workshop manual (very clear
and understandable for the DIY mechanic) is still available at autojumbles, and brand
new from the specialists.

Just as important as whether you can keep on top of maintenance is another
question – will you actually enjoy riding the bike? Riding a Commando is a very
different experience to that of a modern machine. The clutch will seem heavy
(though a carefully routed teflon-lined cable helps a lot), and the gearchange slow
and deliberate. However, these are still good fun bikes to ride.

Let's take power delivery first: Norton's air-cooled parallel twin had its roots
in 1949 as a modest 500, so when the Commando arrived it was already quite
long-in-the-tooth. Despite that, it remains a lusty, likeable engine with plenty of
mid-range torque. The paper power figures of 50-65bhp suggest the performance

A well used and well loved Commando, used for continental touring.

of a mere 500, but that only tells half the story. All Commandos have usable power from 2500-3000rpm, with strong mid-range power right up to 6000-7000. They're easily fast enough to cope with modern traffic, and the 850s, in particular, are relaxed at speed.

There's a definite difference in character between the 750 and 850. The early Commando was relatively lightweight, at less than 400lb for the basic Roadster. It's the sportier option, built when Norton was still trying to keep up with the new generation of superbikes from Japan. By the time the 850 appeared in 1973, the company had accepted that this wasn't possible, and the bigger Commando was detuned, with the emphasis on stamina rather than outright power. It has even more mid-range than the 750, but according to road test figures is actually slower. That's partly down to middle-aged spread – extra equipment saw the Commando's weight balloon to 492lb for the final MkIII, and really transformed from a speed-hungry sportster into a more easy-going tourer. It's telling that most 850s were ordered in touring Interstate form, with the big fuel tank.

Don't expect modern braking performance either. The early Commando's front drum works well when properly set up, while the single Lockheed disc that followed it was OK by 1972 standards, but 'wooden' and not that powerful in the 21st century. This can be much improved with a smaller master cylinder, and there are several other brake upgrades available from the specialists.

Lots has been written about the Commando's handling, and it does have an inherent high-speed weave that didn't affect the company's earlier frame, the Featherbed. Keep within speed limits, and you are unlikely to experience it – it's not dangerous in any case, and doesn't affect road holding. It is important to keep the isolastics properly adjusted for decent handling, though. These should be checked every 2500 miles. If they need adjusting, it's a laborious process on pre-MkIII bikes, using shims. The MkIIIs (1975 on, engine number 325001) used a far superior vernier adjustment system, which made the job quicker and simpler – it's readily available from the specialists, and is easily retro-fitted to older bikes.

Kickstarting a Commando doesn't require bulging thigh muscles, so long as the engine is in tip-top condition and has electronic ignition. The final MkIII had an electric start, but it's often referred to (even in the factory literature!) as an 'electric assist,' as it wasn't quite strong enough to turn over the big twin from cold. However, a four-brush conversion for the motor, plus a bigger amp/hour battery, works wonders.

In short, the Commando really does deliver as the authentic British bike. Given care and attention, plus the improved components now available, it makes for a fun and practical classic bike.

850s were heavier and less-sporting. Few came with this Roadster fuel tank.

4 Relative values
– which model for you?

See Chapter 12 for value assessment. This chapter shows, in percentage terms, the value of individual models in good condition, relative to the Roadster/Interstate 750. There were many variations on the Commando theme, and this chapter also looks at the strengths and weaknesses of each model, so that you can decide which is best for you.

Basically, the Commando's evolution can be divided into two stages: 750 and 850, though there were plenty of changes within each group. One word of warning: Norton tended to make changes on an ongoing basis, with some made mid-year, and not always using consecutive engine numbers, so specific numbers are no guarantee that a particular bike will have a particular feature. The 'Mk' designations can also be confusing on the 750 – the 1971 Fastback, for example, was a MkIII, but the Roadster (to the same spec) was a MkII.

Finally, although the array of Commando models seems bewildering, they are actually very similar under the skin. Norton learned early on that a change of seat, tank and handlebars could create a different bike. The exceptions are the police-spec Interpol and Production Racer, both of which had substantial differences from the standard bikes.

Range availability

Commando 750

1968-72	Fastback
1969-70	S type
1969	R type
1969-73	Interpol
1970-73	Roadster
1971	SS type
1971	Fastback LR
1971-73	Hi-Rider

1972-73	Interstate
1970-72	Production Racer

Commando 850

1973-74	Roadster
1973-74	Hi-Rider
1973-78	Interstate
1973-78	Interpol
1974-75	John Player Special

Commando 750

The 750 is the purist's Commando, especially in early Fastback form. It's lighter than the 850, and the Fastback, in particular, isn't associated with the later troubles of the Combat (see below) Starting from engine number 126125, the prefix 20M3 confirms a MkI 1968 bike, as does the external rev counter drive, with ignition points behind the cylinder barrel. For a real rarity, look out for a 'P' engine number suffix. This denotes the very first batches of bikes built at Norton's old Plumstead factory, which are thought to be better quality than later machines assembled at Andover. Valve covers, footrest supports, gearlever and kickstart all have a rough sandcast finish on the Plumstead bikes – these were polished on later machines. If you come across an original Plumstead-built machine, with that 'P' engine suffix, then that's a real find, and well worth buying if the price is right. Another identification of a 1968 Commando (the Fastback name didn't actually appear until '69) was the use of a circular tank badge on some bikes, instead of the familiar 'Norton' script – these are now extremely rare. Bikes produced up to March 1969 were fitted with the older Dominator-type silencers. The familiar 'peashooter' silencers replaced them, and were fitted up to September 1973. Engine numbers 134108 onwards are post-Plumstead.

The MkI Fastback is a distinctive looking bike, with its combination of straight lines and inclined engine. A few of them had a good-looking twin-tone tank finish. The twin-leading shoe front drum brake works well, but only if set up by someone competent to do the work. For its rarity, this earliest Commando is worth more in original condition than with obvious modifications.

Another distinctive Commando was the Interpol, designed specifically for the police. Offered from 1969, it was one of the longest running models, lasting right up to 1976, and became virtually the standard machine for UK police forces for a time. The exact specification of the Interpol depended on each customer, but a typical police bike had a full fairing, solo seat, and fibreglass panniers, with an all-white finish. Many were sold, but few have survived in their original form. Well worth seeking out as something different, but the blue lights, siren and radio equipment will all have been removed before the bike was sold back into civvy street!

Early in 1970, from engine number 131257, the Fastback was joined by the more conventional-looking Roadster (it did without the rear bodywork) and the S type, with its higher bars and high-level pipes. The S was aimed at the US market, in the street scrambler style, and a proper eyeful it was too. Alongside it was the R type, with similar styling but lower pipes, and a small 2.25-gallon fuel tank in blue or red – rarely seen now, most of these bikes were exported to the USA. These MkII Commandos (though the Roadster is a MkI), have engine prefix 20M3S, and the points were moved to the timing cover and the rev counter drive to the front of the engine.

Original spec 1968 Commando – note circular tank badge and Dominator silencers. (Courtesy Grant Doak)

Pre-Combat 750 with front drum brake.

Bright yellow, high pipes ... a 750S contrasts with the more sober Nortons.

There were several changes the following year: new forks without gaiters, and the new yokes were non-adjustable. One obvious visual change was to the chunky

Roadster 750: small tank and high bars.

Lucas alloy switchgear, which allowed for optional direction indicators. The centre stand now pivoted on the engine plates rather than the frame itself, which was more robust but made checking the isolastics even more tricky than before.

There were more new models as well. The Fastback gained a new variant, the Long Range, or LR, whose chief difference was a big 4-gallon steel fuel tank in place of the standard bike's 3.25-gallon fibreglass item. It also had a conventional seat, lacking the original Fastback's padded wings extending each side of the tank. Only around 400 Fastback LRs were built, many going to Australia, so it's a very rare bike in both Europe and North America. Not that its 'unique' parts *were* unique – the tank was derived from that of the police-spec Interpol, another example of Norton making imaginative use of existing components. In the same vein, the new SS Type was really the high-pipe S, with its exhausts running one each side of the bike rather than both on the left. It was built within engine numbers 145234 and 150723.

The joker in the pack for 1971 was the Hi-Rider; a chopper-inspired factory custom that came complete with ape-hanger bars and extra thick, upswept seat. The Hi-Rider has attracted plenty of ridicule over the years, and few have survived in their original form. That makes them rare and collectable in the 21st century, so if the style appeals and you find one, Norton's chopper is well worth a look. It was part of the range for several years, so evidently some people liked it.

Now, if there's one thing that strikes horror into the hearts of Commando owners, it's the name 'Combat.' In an attempt to boost performance, in early 1972 Norton launched a hopped-up version of the 750 twin, with 10:1 compression, high-lift cam, and bigger (32mm) carburettors. Look for engine numbers over 200000 with the letter 'C' stamped on the cylinder head, just in front of the head steady. The Combat's cylinder barrel was black, and the top barrel fin and lowest cylinder fin are closer together than on a standard Commando. With a claimed 65bhp, the Combat-engined Commandos were certainly fast, though not for very long.

The extra power and stress proved too much for the venerable motor – pistons broke up and main bearings could fail in as little as 3000 miles. Then there were valve gear problems, because the cylinder head had been skimmed to obtain that higher compression ratio, but the pushrods hadn't been shortened to suit. Inexplicably, Norton stopped fitting a sump oil filter at the same time, which made matters worse. And lower gearing cut acceleration times, but made the vulnerable engine rev higher at speed. The Combat, which soon became standard across the range, was a disaster, and more than anything else gave the Commando a reputation for serious unreliability.

Happily, Norton did find a solution. In July '72, a new roller main bearing named 'Superblend' cured the bottom end trouble, and for 1973 the company drew a line under the whole experience by detuning the engine again and fitting higher gearing, as well as a car-type cartridge oil filter.

The Combat's disastrous reputation is no reason to shy away from a '72 Commando, though. Thirty-five years later, it's highly likely that any troublesome bottom end will have been sorted out – according to one specialist, it's now very seldom that a Commando turns up without the requisite Superblend main bearings. With a Superblend bottom end, lower compression, and without the Combat's SS cam, there's no reason why a 1972 Commando shouldn't be as long-lived as any other.

1972 also saw the introduction of the Interstate, with its 5.25-gallon tank (which soon grew to a massive 5.5 gallons) and Lockheed front disc brake (officially an option, but standard in practice). Geometry changes meant that the front end was lightened, probably too much for precise handling. Another couple of general identifiers are that from '72 the engine had no prefix, and the engine breather was moved from the left-hand end of the camshaft to between the gearbox plates behind the engine.

Those much improved 750s, complete with Superblends, oil filter and detuned engine, were designated MkV for 1973, and started with engine number 220000. They also used the Lucas 10CA ignition points – the early 6CA type was a weak unit whose auto-advance could jam on full advance, disaster for a highly tuned Combat. Other identifiers for the '73 750s were black instrument cases, a standard front disc brake, and a big square rear light.

For some, these MkVs are the ultimate Commando 750s. They are heavier than the earlier bikes (especially in Interstate form) but with a Superblend bottom end and lower compression were reliable, and carried the benefits of five years' gradual improvement. They come in Roadster, Interstate and Hi-Rider guise only, as the Fastback was dropped in '72. These final 750s continued in production up to October 1973, alongside the new 850. The last engine was number 230935.

Strengths/weaknesses: The 750 is the sporting option, lighter and, in most cases, faster than the 850. The front drum brake needs either careful setting up, or uprating, and the 750 Commandos lack the many practical improvements that the 850 brought. Combat troubles should have long since been cured. Still a fast, exciting bike to ride.
750 Roadster/Interstate: 100%
750 Fastback: 117%

Commando 850

The Commando 850, despite looking almost identical to the 750, represented a complete break, and although most of the cycle parts remained the same, the engine was thoroughly reworked. It represented a determined attempt by the factory to improve reliability, oil tightness, and stamina. To this end (and in the aftermath of the Combat fiasco) the engine was detuned with a 7.7:1 compression ratio and a milder cam. Norton claimed 60bhp at 6000rpm, but magazine tests revealed a true figure of around 52bhp. It certainly produced less power than the 750, and with the 850's extra weight, explains why these 'bigger' Commandos are generally slower than the 'smaller' ones. Top speed fell to around 111mph, though the 850 still offered a good amount of torque at lower speeds.

The 850 MkI was launched in March 1973, available as an Interstate, Roadster, Hi-Rider, and Interpol, all with standard front disc brake and indicators. The most obvious visual identifiers are the balance pipe between the two exhaust downpipes, a silver cylinder barrel and twin pinstripes on the fuel tank. Engine numbers jumped again, starting at 300000.

Behind the visuals was an engine bored out to 828cc, with a strengthened bottom end (Superblend main bearings, of course) and long bolts clamping cylinder block to crankcase. There were stronger pistons, the crankcase oil filter reappeared (in addition to the existing cartridge filter), and several measures were aimed at eliminating oil leaks.

The rest of the bike wasn't neglected either: stronger gearbox, better quality fork stanchion chrome, a stronger centre stand – that stand finally consigned the 750's flimsy, twisting item to history – and sintered bronze clutch friction plates.

The John Player Norton is a rare variant.

A real one-off: Commando 850 with Difazio front end.

Most 850s had the big Interstate fuel tank. This is a Roadster.

The 850 Interstate makes for a good relaxed touring bike.

The steering head angle was increased by 1 degree in an attempt to cure front end lightness, and the swing arm and rear suspension mountings beefed up. The old Commando bugbear of exhausts coming loose in the cylinder head was also tackled. All of these changes added up to a far more robust machine – heavier and slower than the 750, but more capable of staying in one piece.

In September 1973, from engine 306591, the MkIA 850 was launched, with changes purely aimed at meeting new European noise regulations – hence the large black airbox and new upswept silencers with black mutes poking out of the ends. Referred to as 'black caps' or 'bean cans', for years these pipes were blamed for restricting power, but it's a myth – they don't, though the big airbox does. Candy Apple Red was a new colour option at the same time, alongside the traditional black/gold and silver.

Soon afterwards, the John Player Special was launched. Originally intended for a special short-stroke 750, this used exactly the same running gear as the production 850, but with a big twin-headlight endurance-style fairing, rearset footrests, low bars and solo seat. The JPN capitalised on Norton's racing successes, but was no faster than the standard Commando and has an uncompromising riding position. Only around 200 were made, and they remain a rare variant today. It's thought that another 2500 or so replica JPNs have been converted from standard Commandos since then. An original JPN should come with a factory certificate confirming its authenticity. As for the short-stroke 750 engines, a few of these were built for homologation, to be eligible for production racing – they are very rare. The engine number prefix is 235.

For the MkIIA for 1974 (from engine 307311), the engine reverted to a black barrel and the range remained Roadster, Interstate, Hi-Rider and Interpol. The Interstate's tank was reduced to 4.5 gallons (which made it less uncomfortably wide for the rider's knees), and a new colour option for the Roadster was white with distinctive blue and red stripes. Instruments with the NVT 'wiggly worm' logo are good identifiers, as are fork gaiters. The MkIIA for Europe carried the black cap silencers and big air box, while the plain MkII for USA retained the older cans and airbox.

The final Commando variant was the 850 MkIII, launched in 1975 when Norton was close to bankruptcy. Once again, the emphasis was on making the bike quieter, more civilised and easier to ride. It had electric start, front and rear disc brakes, and (in line with US legislation) a left-foot gearchange, and there were nearly 140 detail changes. The civilian range was narrowed to Roadster and Interstate (most were the latter) though it's thought that a few MkIII JPNs were built as well.

There isn't room here to cover all the MkIII changes, but the primary drive chain gained an hydraulic tensioner, and its cover was now secured by twelve small screws to make it more oil-tight. The age-old problem of oil draining into the sump when the bike was standing was addressed with an anti-drain valve in the timing cover. The electric start tackled another perceived fault, but wasn't up to the job (though it can be, see below) and the isolastics gained a vernier adjustment system that made checking clearances far quicker and easier. Uprated electrics and improved exhaust-to-head joints were other changes.

With weight now up to 492lb, lower compression and higher gearing, the 850MkIII was probably the slowest Commando of all, with a top speed of around 105mph. On the other hand, it was more reliable, oil-tight and robust than any of its predecessors, very different in character to any of the 750s, a solid, torquey tourer, able to cross Europe two-up with a pile of luggage.

Strengths/weaknesses: The 850 is a stronger bike than the 750 all round, with lots of worthwhile improvements. There's more mid-range but actually less top-end power, and higher gearing makes it more relaxed. The pay-off is more weight and a less sporting character, but judging by prices that's something many riders are happy to live with.

850 Roadster/Interstate: 114%
850 JPN (genuine): 250%

Production Racer

The rarest Commando of all. The Production Racer was a limited edition replica of Norton's own race bikes, road legal but ready to race. Just 119 were built between 1970 and '72, all assembled at the Norton Villiers Performance Shop, next to the Thruxton race circuit in Hampshire.

Compared to a standard Commando, the Production Racer came with that can't-miss-it bright yellow bodywork, clip-ons and rearsets. There were alloy wheel rims, tucked in exhaust system, and an adjustable isolastic head steady in place of the standard fixed rubber mount. An 11.5in disc brake replaced the front drum, and the rear drum gained top and bottom vents. The engine internals were polished, with 10.5:1 compression and Double S camshaft.

The only difficulty in buying a Production Racer is ensuring that it's genuine. There was no special engine or frame prefix, and replica bodywork has been available for some time, allowing any Commando to be turned into a Racer lookalike. The only way to be sure is to contact Norman White (see Chapter 17 for contact details) – he worked at the Performance Shop, and has build records for every bike.

Production Racer (genuine): 380%

Any guesses why the Production Racer was nicknamed 'Yellow Peril'?

5 Before you view
– be well informed

To avoid a wasted journey, and the disappointment of finding that the bike does not match your expectations, it will help if you're very clear about what questions you want to ask before you pick up the phone. Some of these points might appear basic, but when you're excited about the prospect of buying your dream classic, it's amazing how some of the most obvious things slip the mind ... Also, check the current values of the model in which you're interested in the classic bike magazine classified ads.

Where is the bike?
Is it going to be worth travelling to the next county/state, or even across a border? A locally advertised machine, although it may not sound very interesting, can add to your knowledge for very little effort, so make a visit – it might even be in better condition than expected.

Dealer or private sale?
Establish early on if the bike is being sold by its owner or by a trader. A private owner should have all the history, so don't be afraid to ask detailed questions. A dealer may have more limited knowledge of the bike's history, but should have some documentation. A dealer may offer a warranty/guarantee (ask for a printed copy).

Cost of collection and delivery?
A dealer may well be used to quoting for delivery. A private owner may agree to meet you halfway, but only agree to this after you have seen the bike at the vendor's address to validate the documents. Conversely, you could meet halfway and agree the sale, but insist on meeting at the vendor's address for the hand-over.

View – when and where?
It's always preferable to view at the vendor's home or business premises. In the case of a private sale, the bike's documentation should tally with the vendor's name and address. Arrange to view only in daylight, and avoid a wet day – the vendor may be reluctant to let you take a test ride if it's wet.

Reason for sale?
Do make it one of the first questions. Why is the bike being sold and how long has it been with the current owner? How many previous owners?

Condition?
Ask for an honest appraisal of the bike's condition. Ask specifically about some of the check items described in Chapter 8.

All original specification
A completely original Commando will be worth more than a modified one,

but certain mods (electronic ignition, bigger disc brake) can also indicate a conscientious owner who has been actively riding/caring for the machine.

Matching data/legal ownership?

Do frame, engine numbers and licence plate match the official registration document? Is the owner's name and address recorded there, too?

For those countries that require an annual test of roadworthiness, does the bike have a document showing it complies (an MoT certificate in the UK, which can be verified on 0845 600 5977)?

If it's a 1975 or later bike, does it carry a current road fund license/license plate tag? Earlier bikes are road tax exempt in the UK.

Does the vendor own the bike outright? Money might be owed to a finance company or bank: the bike could even be stolen. Several organisations will supply the data on ownership, based on the bike's licence plate number, for a fee. Such companies can often also tell you whether the bike has been 'written off' by an insurance company. In the UK these organisations can supply vehicle data:

HPI – 01722 422 422 – www.hpicheck.com
AA – 0870 600 0836 – www.theaa.com
RAC – 0870 533 3660 – www.rac.co.uk

Other countries will have similar organisations.

Unleaded fuel?

Has the bike been modified to run on unleaded fuel? A tuned high-compression Commando will need an octane booster additive to keep it happy.

Insurance

Check with your existing insurer before setting out – your current policy might not cover you if you do buy the bike and decide to ride it home.

How can you pay?

A cheque/check will take several days to clear, and the seller may prefer to sell to a cash buyer. However, a banker's draft (a cheque issued by a bank) is as good as cash, but safer, so contact your own bank and become familiar with the formalities that are necessary to obtain one.

Buying at auction?

If the intention is to buy at auction see Chapter 10 for further advice.

Professional vehicle check (mechanical examination)

There are often marque/model specialists who will undertake professional examination of a vehicle on your behalf. Owners clubs may be able to put you in touch with such specialists.

6 Inspection equipment

– these items will really help

This book
Reading glasses (if you need them for close work)
Overalls
Digital camera
Compression tester
A friend, preferably a knowledgeable enthusiast

Before you rush out of the door, gather together a few items that will help as you work your way around the bike. This book is designed to be your guide at every step, so take it along and use the check boxes in chapter 9 to help you assess each area of the bike. Don't be afraid to let the seller see you using it.

Take your reading glasses if you need them to read documents and make close up inspections.

Be prepared to get dirty. Take along a pair of overalls, if you have them. A digital camera is handy so that later you can study some areas of the bike more closely. Take a picture of any part of the bike that causes you concern, and seek an expert opinion.

A compression tester is easy to use. It screws into the spark plug holes (on a Commando these couldn't be easier to get to). With the ignition off, turn the engine over on full throttle to get the compression reading.

Ideally, have a friend or knowledgeable enthusiast accompany you: a second opinion is always valuable.

7 Fifteen minute evaluation
– walk away or stay?

General condition

Put the bike on its centre stand, to shed equal light on both sides, and take a good, slow walk around it. If it's claimed to be restored, and has a nice shiny tank and engine cases, look more closely – how far does the 'restored' finish go? Are the nooks and crannies behind the gearbox as spotless as the fuel tank? If not, the bike may have been given a quick smarten up prior to going on sale. A generally faded look all over isn't necessarily a bad thing – it suggests a machine that hasn't been restored, and isn't trying to pretend that it has.

Now look at the engine – by far the most expensive and time-consuming thing to put right if anything's wrong. A lot of people will have told you that all old Nortons leak oil, but there shouldn't be any leaks if the engine is in good condition and has been put together well. It shouldn't be spattered with lube, or have oily drips underneath. Even if it's dry on top, get down on your knees and have a peek at the underside of the crankcase – nice and dry, or covered in oil?

Take the bike off the centre stand and start the engine – it should fire up within two or three kicks, and rev up crisply and cleanly without showing blue or black smoke. If it's an 850 MkIII, see if the electric start works. Listen for rumbles and knocks from the bottom end and primary drive – any of these are precursors to serious work. While the engine's running, check that the ignition light or ammeter show that the electrics are charging.

Switch the engine off and put the bike back on its centre stand. Check for play in the forks, headstock and swingarm. Are there leaks from the front forks or rear shocks? Are details like the seat, badges and tank colour right for the year of the bike? (A little research helps here, and the reference books listed at the end of this volume have all this information.)

Spotting a fake

Since most Commando variants differed only in fuel tank, handlebars, seats or exhausts, it's relatively easy to change the identity of a machine by bolting on the relevant bits. Nothing wrong with that, so long as it's made clear by the seller that this is the case. If you're offered a Fastback Long Range, ask for proof that it's an original, not a standard Fastback with the LR's tank and seat. John Player Nortons are also easy to fake – there are many more replicas around than genuine bikes, which should come with their original factory certificate.

This gets more serious with the 1970-72 Production Racer, produced in very limited numbers and worth considerably more than a standard Commando. Because original bikes didn't have special engine or frame numbers, it's tricky to tell an original from a fake. Commando specialists Les Emery and Mick Hemmings have built brand new replicas, but they will have records to confirm the provenance of 'their' bikes. Norman White, who worked on the original Production Racers, is the best person to judge whether or not one of these bikes is genuine.

Again, there's nothing wrong with a replica LR, JPN or Production Racer, so long as you know what you're buying, and don't pay over the odds for it.

Documentation

If the seller claims to be the bike's owner, make sure he/she really is by checking the registration document, which, in the UK, is the V5C. The person listed on the V5 isn't necessarily the legal owner, but their details should match those of whoever is selling the bike. Also, use the V5C to check the engine/frame numbers.

An annual roadworthiness certificate – the 'MoT' in the UK – is handy proof not just that the bike was roadworthy when tested, but, if there's a whole sheaf of them, gives evidence of the bike's history, when it was actively being used, and what the mileage was. The more of these that come with the bike, the better.

Do the engine and frame numbers tally with the documentation?

On pre-1974 bikes, engine/frame numbers should match.

Put the bike on its centre stand and have a good, slow walk around it.

The engine should be mechanically quieter than other British twins.

8 Key points

– where to look for problems

One of the most important aspects of the bike – the owner. How long have they had the Commando? How knowledgeable are they? Do they have a decent range of tools, and are they are a member of the Norton Owners Club? A knowledgeable, conscientious owner is one of the surest signs of a good, well cared for machine.

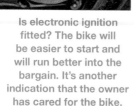

Is electronic ignition fitted? The bike will be easier to start and will run better into the bargain. It's another indication that the owner has cared for the bike.

The engine number is a good indication of when the bike was made and what production improvements it has. However, it gives an 'indication' only, as Norton sometimes built engines into bikes out of sequence.

Check that the finned locking rings holding the exhaust downpipes into the head are tight. If they're loose (or worse still, left loose while the bike is ridden) they will allow the pipes to vibrate in the head and strip the threads in the exhaust port (the only cure involves removing the head and having helicoils fitted).

Check the swingarm for play. The bushes are often neglected, and the spindle itself can wear. In that case, the only cure is to remove the engine and swingarm and ream out the bushes and engine/gearbox cradle to accept an oversize spindle. Not a five minute job.

24

9 Serious evaluation

– 30 minutes for years of enjoyment

Score each section as follows: 4 = excellent; 3 = good; 2 = average; 1 = poor
The totting up procedure is detailed at the end of the chapter. Be realistic in your marking!

Engine/frame numbers   ④ ③ ② ①

Engine and frame numbers are good clues as to when the bike was built, and thus what production improvements it may have benefited from. They are only an indication, though, as Norton sometimes used engines or frames out of sequence, and improvements tended to be made throughout the year rather than all in one go for each new model year. Nevertheless, they are a very useful guide.

Engine number indicates age – this is a late 850 MkII or IIA.

The engine number is clearly visible on the left-hand base of the cylinder barrel, and the frame number is on a riveted plate on the steering head – you'll have to push some cables aside to read the frame number, and the plate also shows date and place of manufacture. Engine and frame numbers should match (up to 1974, that is – after that, the frames went out of sequence). If the numbers do match, then that's a bonus, confirmation that the bike has its original engine and frame. Of course, it's not the end of the world if they don't match – you could still have a perfectly fine motorcycle (and some bikes left the factory like that).

The frame number is on the steering head.

From 1973, many Commandos used an Italian-built frame, and some of these have proved to be somewhat fragile at the rear, but any such problems should have been long since sorted out. There were some British frames as well, when the Italians couldn't keep up with production. A frame number prefix 'F' indicates an Italian or British frame from this era. If there's no 'F' prefix, then the frame is British. Gearboxes are also numbered (unless they've been rebuilt with a new shell), and a 'C' stamped on top of the cylinder head denotes a Combat engine. Engine prefix 20M3 indicates a MkI, and should only be found on a Fastback or early Interpol; 20M3S means a MkII Commando. A 'P' suffix denotes one of the very early Plumstead-built bikes; a rare find indeed.

The gearbox number is at the rear of the box, visible from above.

'C' = Combat.

Paint   ④ ③ ② ①

In the author's opinion, most Commandos are less flashy than contemporary Triumphs, for example, but they're handsome

A good respray is a beautiful thing.

bikes nonetheless, and a lot of that is down to the paintwork. Traditional black/gold or silver/black are favourites, especially for Interstates, but the metallic reds and blues look good, too.

Not that there's much of it – the good news about restoring any old bike is that there's not a lot of bodywork to paint. In the Commando's case this extends to the tank, side panels, and (in the case of the Fastback) tailpiece – mudguards were always unpainted, in chrome or stainless steel.

The finish generally holds up well, but don't underestimate the cost of a professional respray, which is well worth having done, as the fuel tank, in particular, is such a focal point of the bike. Look for evidence of quick and cheap resprays, and that the pinstriping is even and hasn't been worn away. Light staining around the filler cap from spilt fuel might polish out, but could also require a respray.

Generally speaking, faded original paintwork isn't such a bad thing, and, in fact, many riders prefer this unrestored look – there are so many shiny restored Commandos around that an honest-looking original, even if it a little faded around the edges, has its own appeal.

Chrome ④ ③ ② ①

There's a lot of chrome on the Commando: fork stanchions, wheel rims, early mudguards, handlebars, exhaust system, headlamp, and numerous other bits and pieces. The factory finish wasn't the best, and the chrome would actually peel off early wheel rims, though like many other issues with the production line quality, this should have been dealt with by now.

Shiny. There's nothing like good chrome.

The fork stanchions on 750s are another problem area, and if the chrome pits or starts flaking here it's more than just a cosmetic problem, as no oil seal can cope with a rough surface for long, and the forks will start to leak. Commando 850s have better quality fork chrome, so they're less likely to have a problem, and some MkIIs and IIIs had gaiters as well, which helps.

Whichever bike you're looking at, check the chrome for rust, pitting, and general dullness. Minor blemishes can be polished away, but otherwise you're looking at a replating bill. If the silencers are seriously pitted, it's a better idea to budget for a new pair – less hassle than getting the old ones replated.

Tinwork ④ ③ ② ①

Pity the poor car buyer for the acres of bodywork and tucked away crevices to check for rust and rot. On a bike, especially an old bike like the Commando, life is far simpler, with bodywork restricted to fuel tank, mudguards, side panels, and the Fastback's tail unit.

The Fastback, of course, used fibreglass for its tank, panels and tail unit, and this should be checked for cracks and glazing. It can be repaired, or a good respray may be sufficient, but if the bodywork is too far gone, new replacements are

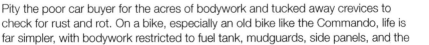

available. The Fastback Long Range (if you can find one) used a steel tank. The early Roadster and Interstate used a fibreglass tank as well, until the UK authorities outlawed non-metal tanks. Fibreglass tanks were finally phased out in 1974.

Steel tanks should be checked for leaks around the tap and along the seams, as well as for dents and rust. Watch out for patches of filler. Minor leaks can sometimes be repaired with Petseal, but for welded repairs you'll have to flush out the tank (which has to be thorough, you don't want any petrol vapour hanging around when the welding torch is fired up) but the fuel tank is at least easy to remove.

Check the tinwork for dents and scratches ...

... and if you find any, it's a good bargaining counter.

Side panels were either fibreglass or steel, depending on model, and again these are available as new spares, so it's not a disaster if they're missing – though that should be reflected in the price, as their absence makes any bike look tatty and incomplete. You wouldn't have thought a simple panel had such an impact, but it does.

Commando mudguards have always been steel – chrome on the early 750s, stainless steel on the MkV 750 and all 850s. They should be straight and (not a problem on the stainless guards, of course) rust-free.

Transfers

The Commando had no screwed-on badges, like a Triumph or BSA, and instead the Norton and Commando badges on the tank and side panels were stick-on. They are the finishing touch to any machine, but it's not a problem if they're peeling off or have letters missing, because new

New transfers are available.

The 850 MkIII in silver used black badges.

ones are available. Commando specialists, the Vintage Motorcycle Club's transfer scheme and the Norton Owners Club will be able to help with new badges.

Seat

You'd be forgiven for thinking that a seat is just a seat, but the various Commandos used a whole variety of shapes and sizes, according to model. Interpol, John Player Special and Production Racer all had solo seats, and the others dual seats.

Original quilted seat on an 850.

Splits and holes will let in water.

At its public launch, the Fastback had an orange seat, though, perhaps fortunately, this never made it to production. When the bike went on sale, it was with a plain black seat, smooth finish, with a grabstrap for the passenger. Most of the others featured quilted or otherwise patterned seats, all with a passenger strap. The arrival of the 850 brought thicker padding, and only the Fastback had a rear hump and those curious padded wings either side of the fuel tank. The prize for most distinctive seat must go to the Hi-Rider, whose thick upswept item would have been interesting for any passenger – curiously reminiscent of the Raleigh Chopper bicycle, of the same era.

Whichever type of seat the bike has, the points to look for are the same. Fibreglass seat pans can actually rust, and metal ones *will* rust, and eventually give way, though this is easy enough to check – unscrew the two large knurled knobs and the seat lifts off complete, except on 850 MkIIIs, which have a hinged seat.

Covers can split, which, of course, allows rain in, which the foam padding soaks up ... and never dries out. That's a recipe for a permanently wet backside, or a rock hard seat on frosty mornings (the author speaks from bitter experience). New seats are available, but not all of them, though any seat specialist will be able to restore the one you've got, whatever its condition.

Rubbers

Worn footrest rubbers are a sign of high mileage, though as they're so cheap and easy to replace, not an infallible one. They should be secure on the footrest and free of splits or tears. If the footrest itself is bent upwards, that's a sure sign the bike has been down the road at some point, so look for other telltale signs on that side. The kickstart and gearchange rubbers are also easy to replace, so well worn ones could indicate neglect. On kickstart bikes, beware the worn smooth rubber – your foot's liable to slip off while kicking the bike over, with painful results as the kickstart lever slams back into your leg. The rubber should also be firm on the lever and not drop off after half a dozen kicks. Of course, if the engine needs that many kicks to fire it up, then something's wrong there anyway.

Footrest rubbers are easily replaced.

Frame

All Commandos used the same basic steel spine frame, but this was changed almost annually as Norton made small improvements here and there. Very early frames could break at the steering head gusset, but an extra horizontal tube cured that. Any problems with the Italian-built frames (see above) should have been dealt with by now. The 850 frame and fork yokes, with their different geometry, are thought to deliver more positive high speed handling.

A frame that is really shabby will necessitate a strip down and repaint or powder coat, though, as with the other paintwork, if it's original and fits with the patina of the bike, then there's a good case for leaving it as it is. The oil tank mounting rubbers can fail, especially if they've been contaminated with oil (it happens ...) or were originally fitted twisted (which also happens). If they do, it puts all the strain on the lower fixing, which eventually splits from the tank altogether.

The same basic frame served all the Commandos.

The most important job is to check whether the main frame is straight and true. Crash damage may have bent it, putting the wheels out of line. One way of checking is by an experienced eye, string and a straight

The frame downtubes are the easiest to examine for rust and flaky paint.

edge, but the surest way to ascertain a frame's straightness is on the test ride – any serious misalignment should be obvious in the way the bike handles. Consistently pulling to one side is a sure sign that either frame or forks are bent.

850 centre stands (like this one) are stronger.

Stands

☐4 ☐3 ☐2 ☐1

All Commandos were fitted with both centre and side stands. Both should be secure and not allow the bike to wobble about. The 750 1971/72 side stand is notoriously weak, and the factory later introduced a repair/reinforcement mounting kit. If the bike leans over too far on the side stand, this kit can be fitted, or, better still, the later weld-on tab mounting for the stand. Check the 750 centre stand as well; they weren't really strong enough and could twist. This applies to both 1969-70 stands mounted directly on the frame, and the '71 on stands bolted to the engine plates. The later arrangement gave more cornering clearance but does make checking the rear isolastic more difficult.

The 850 centre stand is far better and stronger, and solved the problem of checking the rear isolastic. It's available new and will fit all 1971-on Commandos with the engine plate mounting.

Lights

☐4 ☐3 ☐2 ☐1

All Commandos had reasonable lights, thanks to the 12-volt alternator electrics, and from 1973 (750 MkV) Norton fitted a halogen headlight bulb. Thanks to the isolastics, Commandos are less prone to blowing bulbs than some other British

Check that all the lights work.

classics, but it can happen, so check that headlight, rear light and brake light all work. Ditto the indicators, though the early Lucas flashers don't always flash as intended.

There were two styles of rear light, the small pointed one up to 1972, and the big square one from '73 onwards, fitted to both 750 and 850. In either case an LED bulb replacement is worth considering, as it's 'fit and forget'.

The Commando, like its British contemporaries, has just one fuse.

Electrics/wiring 〔4〕 〔3〕 〔2〕 〔1〕

The Commando's 12-volt alternator electrics are fairly reliable, though the Lucas coils, ballast resistor and contact breaker points can all fail over time. Two distinctive features are (from 1971) capacitor ignition, which meant the bike could be started and ridden without a battery (or if the battery was flat ...) and an auxiliary power socket for powering an inspection light or shaver – the latter for midnight breakdowns or if you desperately need a shave while out for a ride in the country. More to the point, it can also be used to charge the battery in situ.

All bikes had twin 6-volt coils.

Some Commandos still retain their contact breaker points. The Lucas 6CA points fitted to early bikes are not good news, the auto-advance liable to wear quickly, deliver a variable gap, and stick on full advance. The 10CA points fitted from 1973 are better, but the real solution is electronic ignition, which is superior in just about every respect. If you're a real stickler for originality, or like fettling with points, you may not agree, but solid-state ignition isn't expensive and is well worth fitting. If a previous owner has taken the trouble to do it, that's a good sign.

Many electrical troubles are simply down to poor earths (grounds) or dodgy connections. The multi-pin sockets used on the MkIII can corrode, while older bullet connectors can be removed and resoldered. Either way, an electrical fault is a good bargaining counter, as many riders see electrics as a form of black art they are reluctant to delve into, even though the fault may be a relatively simple one.

If it's a MkIII, does the electric start work?

Lots has been written about the inadequacies of the 850 MkIII's 'electric assister' electric start, but it can be made to work properly. A 4-brush conversion for the motor, a decent 20 amp/hr battery and thicker cables should do the trick. If the starter won't engage cleanly, then the culprit is likely to be the sprag clutch.

Check for loose or broken spokes.

Tyres last well.

Wheels/tyres

All Commandos used spoked wheels with chromed steel rims (apart from alloy spoked rims on the original Production Racer). Check that the chrome is intact and not pitted or peeling away. Run a screwdriver lightly over the spokes – any that sound 'off' will need tensioning. If any spokes are broken or missing, the bike is unrideable.

Commandos are not hard on tyres – we're used to big modern bikes needing a fresh rear tyre after 4-5000 miles, but then they are dealing with about twice the power of a Commando. Given a gentle rider, rears can last as long as 10,000 miles, and fronts even longer. If the tyre is worn, the legal minimum in the UK is at least 1mm of tread depth across at least three-quarters of the breadth of the tyre.

Because the rubber lasts so long, and because many Commandos cover relatively few miles a year, tyres cracking or going hard is probably more of an issue than straightforward wear. Although easy to sort out, tyre problems are a good bargaining counter and should be reflected in the price you pay. TT100s are still available, and suit the big Norton, and Avon's current Road Rider tyre is thought to be good for the Commando. It's not available as a 19-inch rear, but swapping the wheel for a WM3 x 18 gives a much wider choice of modern tyres.

Wheel bearings

Commandos aren't especially hard on wheel bearings, and the bits themselves aren't expensive. Fitting them is a hassle, though, and badly worn bearings could affect handling, so it's worth checking them out. Put the bike on its centre stand

and, with the steering on full lock, try rocking the front wheel in a vertical plane, then spin the wheel and listen for signs of roughness.

How not to do it on the front wheel – check in the vertical, not horizontal, plane.

With the bike on its centre stand, check for play in the wheel bearings.

Next, grasp the rear wheel (which should be clear of the ground) and repeat the check, but don't mistake movement at the isolastics or swing arm for wheel bearing play.

Steering head bearings

Again, the bearings don't cost an arm or a leg, but trouble here can affect the handling, and changing them is a big job. With the bike on the centre stand and the front wheel clear of the ground, swing the handlebars from lock to lock. They should move freely, with no hint of roughness or stiff patches – if there is, budget for replacements. To check for play, take the bike off the centre stand, hold the front brake on and rock the bike back and forth.

Loose steering head bearings will affect handling.

Swing arm bearings

The swing arm bearings rarely fail if regularly lubed with EP140 oil. The trouble is, the standard grease nipple persuades some owners to use grease instead, which blocks the tiny oil holes and leaves the bushes without any sort of lube. Norton's answer, on 1974-on MkII and III 850s, was to delete the nipple. However, as not much oil was put in at the factory, and the internal wicking arrangements don't work very well, all in all it's likely that a Commando swing arm won't have been properly lubricated throughout its life. To check for play, grasp the rear wheel and try rocking it from side to side – this sounds like the wheel bearing check, but it should be obvious where play is coming from. Don't confuse the prescribed play in the isolastics with swing arm play. To confirm that it is the swing arm, squeeze a couple fingers onto the end of the swing arm pivot, and, if there is play, you'll be able to feel it there as the wheel is rocked. There should be no movement at all. If there is, it could be just worn bushes, but if the entire spindle is loose and rocking in the engine/gearbox cradle, then a new oversize spindle is required, which is a major engine-out job.

The swing arm should be lubed with oil, not grease.

Check for play in the swing arm pivot bushes.

Suspension

All Commandos use the same basic suspension setup: front telescopic forks and twin rear dampers. Early bikes, and MkII/III 850s, had fork gaiters, which is good news, but most original forks were exposed to weather and road salt. Commando 750 fork stanchion chrome is more prone to peeling and pitting than that on the 850, but the bottom line is that forks which are looked after will last well. The same goes for the exposed rear shocks – covers fitted over the top will do a lot to protect them from weather and water.

Check the forks and rear shocks for leaks. If the fork stanchions are pitted, they'll need to be replated and reground to size, or dumped in favour of new ones – there's no point fitting new seals to rough forks. An oil leak will be obvious on exposed forks, but on the gaiter-equipped forks, grasp the gaiter and try rubbing it on the fork leg – if it moves easily, then there's likely to be oil underneath, and you have a leak.

Check the forks for play by holding the bottom of the legs and trying to rock them back and forth – play here indicates worn bushes, and new ones aren't expensive. New rear shocks are available, and Hagons are recommended.

Examine fork stanchions for pitting and leaks. These are perfect.

Gaiters protect the forks, but could still be hiding a leak.

Hagon makes suitable replacement rear shocks.

Also check the lower fork legs for rust, though this is cosmetic only.

Instruments

Commando instruments are what you'd expect from a British classic: speedometer and rev counter, plus the early 750s had an ammeter as well. A few different types were fitted – the earlier Smiths instruments are thought to be more reliable, but even the youngest Commando clock will now be over 30 years old, so expect some wear. Exact replicas of the originals aren't available (though there are some that need only slight modification to the instrument pod), but there are competent repairers out there who will happily recondition a

Original 'green spot' speedo and ammeter.

speedo or rev counter, however old or worn it is.

Engine/gearbox – general impressions

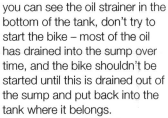

You can tell a lot about the likely condition of a Commando engine without even hearing it run. These engines are deceptively easy to work on, the drawback being that this encourages keen and/or impecunious owners to take things apart themselves, often without the proper tools. Look for chewed-up screws or Allen bolt heads and rounded-off bolts, plus damage to the casings surrounding them. Loose exhaust downpipe locking rings are another sign of poor maintenance.

Ask the owner who maintains the bike, and how often he or she changes the oil – it should be every 2000 miles. What oil do they use? Monograde 50 is best (though not everyone agrees!) – these engines weren't designed for multigrade or synthetic oils. Now, check the oil in the tank – is it nice and clean, or black and sludgy? The latter suggests lots of short journeys, or poor maintenance, or both. If you can see the oil strainer in the bottom of the tank, don't try to start the bike – most of the oil has drained into the sump over time, and the bike shouldn't be started until this is drained out of the sump and put back into the tank where it belongs.

It's part of motorcycling folklore that old British bikes leak oil, but this isn't necessarily the case. As long as the engine is in good condition and has been properly put together with modern sealants, it should be reasonably oil-tight (especially true in the case of the 850). Some light misting isn't a bad sign, but if the bike has a puddle of oil underneath, and the engine/gearbox is covered in lubricant, walk away; unless, of course, the price reflects the condition. An engine like that is likely to need a complete rebuild.

That said, there are some common leak points – from the rev counter drive and kickstart shaft, for example – and some 850s had porous cylinder heads (indicated by a leak from the third fin from the top). An oily air cleaner isn't necessarily bad

Norton's twin is deceptively easy to work on.

Check that the exhaust locking rings are tight – the owner should have the proper C spanner.

It may be tricky to see where leaks are coming from.

Rev counter drive, on the right, is a common leakage spot.

news – oil loss from the tank into the air cleaner is common if the tank is overfilled or the tank breather connections are mistakenly reversed.

Ask the owner if an anti-drain valve has been fitted. These prevent oil draining into the sump when the bike is left unused for long periods. If it's fitted in the oil feed pipe, however, that's bad news, because it will have starved the bearings of oil for several seconds after starting. Wet sumping, as it's known, is best tackled with an 850 MkIII anti-drain valve in the timing cover (these can be retro-fitted to older bikes, with a suitably modified cover). A new oil pump will also help.

You can't really check the gearbox internals at this first look over, but remove the primary chain access cover (not on 850 MkIIIs – they don't have one) rest a finger on the primary chain and then waggle the rear chain up and down. If the primary chain tension changes as you do this, then the clutch sleeve bearing is worn.

An engine in good condition should start first or second kick.

Engine – starting/idling

Before attempting to start the bike, have a peek into the oil tank. If you can see the oil filter/strainer, then leave the kickstart alone – this means the bike has been sitting unused for some time, and most of the oil has drained into the sump. The only answer is to drain the sump and return the oil to the tank.

As mentioned earlier, kickstarting a Commando is more about technique than strength, and an experienced owner should be able start it in one or two kicks. If there's play in the kickstart shaft, then the gearbox layshaft bearing is likely to be the culprit – replacing the bearing with a roller-bearing is the long-term answer, though a special ball-race is also available.

If the bike is an 850 MkIII, ask the owner whether the electric start is in standard spec, or has been upgraded with a four-bush conversion. With that in place, and a beefier battery, it should turn over the engine with no problem. If the starter won't engage, and just whirrs over, then the sprag clutch is worn.

Once started, the engine should settle down to an even, reliable tickover, though if it's from cold, the owner will know exactly how much choke it needs.

The green button is the MkIII's electric start.

Blue smoke indicates
bore wear.

Listen for rumbles
from the bottom end or
primary drive.

Engine – smoke/noise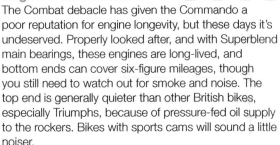

The Combat debacle has given the Commando a poor reputation for engine longevity, but these days it's undeserved. Properly looked after, and with Superblend main bearings, these engines are long-lived, and bottom ends can cover six-figure mileages, though you still need to watch out for smoke and noise. The top end is generally quieter than other British bikes, especially Triumphs, because of pressure-fed oil supply to the rockers. Bikes with sports cams will sound a little noiser.

Ask the owner whether the bike uses oil – it shouldn't need frequent topping-up. A puff of smoke on starting isn't a problem, but if it doesn't clear, the bike could be wet sumping (see above) or simply have been overfilled with oil. The latter can happen because some dipsticks are too short and give a false reading. The dipstick should be five inches long – if it's 3.5 inches long, the level should not be more than a quarter-inch above the 'Low' mark.

Try 'blipping' the throttle – blue smoke indicates bore wear, though this is best tested on the road, under power. Whilst out on the road, smoke when shutting off is due to valve guide wear. Post-1971 guides were fitted with oil seals, so it could be just the seals that need replacing.

Listen out for rumbles and knocks from the bottom end. Pre-Superblend main bearings were notoriously short-lived (and not just on Combats). From engine number 220000, Superblends were fitted at the factory, and since they fit the earlier bikes too, most should now have them. Ask the owner.

Primary drive noise is likely to be
caused by a loose chain.

Primary drive

More noise to listen for – blip the throttle and listen for rumbling from the primary drive. If the chain is worn, it can be adjusted (on pre-MkIIIs) by moving the gearbox backwards. Or it could be low on oil – the oil level hole isn't a good check as it was set too high. The only sure way to get the level right is to refill with a quarter-pint of oil (pre-MkIII) or one-third of a pint (MkIII). Either way, if the oil is low, it's a sign of a careless owner. On the other hand, if the owner has fitted a belt primary drive conversion, then that's good news – not only is the toothed belt quieter and smoother than a chain, it's a sign of an interested, conscientious owner.

MkIII primary chain had an automatic tensioner.

850 MkIIIs were fitted with an hydraulic primary chain tensioner, using the chaincase's own oil supply. These can drain if the bike is left unused for a long time, and the result will be a slack chain, betrayed by a deep rumble when the bike is started. Don't confuse this with main bearing wear – if it gets worse when the throttle is suddenly cracked open, then it's the chain. The MkIII's tensioner will not prime itself by running the bike – rather, it will eventually, but by that time you'll have done serious damage to the transmission. The only answer is to remove the whole chaincase and prime the tensioner by hand.

Well lubed, properly adjusted chain.

Chain/sprockets

With the engine switched off, examine the final drive chain and sprockets. Is the chain clean, well lubed, and properly adjusted? The best way to check how worn it is is to take hold of a link and try to pull it rearwards away from the sprocket. It should only reveal a small portion of the sprocket teeth – any more, and it needs replacing.

Check the rear sprocket teeth for wear – if they have a hooked appearance, the sprocket needs replacing. Ditto if any teeth are damaged or missing. If the rear sprocket needs replacing, then the gearbox sprocket will too. Chains and sprockets aren't massively expensive, but changing the gearbox sprocket takes some dismantling time.

5/08

Battery

Hinge up or lift off the seat and check the battery. Acid splashes indicate overcharging. The correct electrolyte level is a good sign of a meticulous owner, and do check that the battery is held securely in place by its rubber strap. If it can jump around, this strains the cables and it might short out.

The battery is located under the seat.

Engine/gearbox isolastics

The best way to evaluate the isolastics is on the test ride. If the bike wallows on corners, then the system is out of adjustment or needs new rubbers. Either way, it's not a big deal, though a good bargaining counter. The recommended clearance

is 0.006-0.010in, but they can be set loose for a smoother rider, or tighter for tauter handling. The front mounting tends to go out of adjustment first, as it's exposed to the elements.

If the later vernier adjustment system has been fitted to a

This is the heart of the isolastic system.

The front isolastic is exposed to the weather.

pre-MkIII Commando, that's good news – not only does it make adjustment far easier and quicker, but (once again) it's a sign of an owner who takes maintenance seriously.

Exhaust

Check the silencers for rot, both the evident external sort and internal rotting that will be obvious when the engine's fired up. The silencers can also fracture around their captive nuts. It's part of Commando folklore that the black cap cans on MkIA/IIA/

MkIII 850s are highly restrictive, but they're not; it's the airbox that strangles the engine. Also check the downpipes for corrosion, and

(if you haven't already), that the pipes and their locking rings are firm in the exhaust ports.

Check the silencers for rot.

Shapely high pipes on 750S.

Test ride

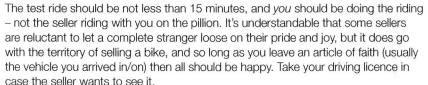

The test ride should be not less than 15 minutes, and *you* should be doing the riding – not the seller riding with you on the pillion. It's understandable that some sellers are reluctant to let a complete stranger loose on their pride and joy, but it does go with the territory of selling a bike, and so long as you leave an article of faith (usually the vehicle you arrived in/on) then all should be happy. Take your driving licence in case the seller wants to see it.

Main warning lights

Warning lights changed over the years. 1968-70 Commandos had just two, plus an ammeter in the headlamp shell. From 1971, the ammeter was dropped, with ignition, main beam and indicator warning lights fitted. The MkIII boasted four: ignition,

indicators, main beam, and even a neutral light. In all cases, the ignition light is a charge warning, and it should extinguish with the engine on a fast idle.

The MkIII's full array.

Engine performance

A Commando in good condition should accelerate crisply and without hesitation. These are still reasonably quick bikes, well able to keep up with (and get past!) modern traffic. There's good torque from 3000rpm (especially on the 850) with 750s giving a power kick from around 5500. That said, you can still make very good progress using no more than 4000-5000rpm. Expect low frequency vibration up to 2500-3000rpm, at which point the isolastics take over and it all smooths out.

If the engine runs unevenly and uses a lot of fuel (though that can't be ascertained on a short

The big twin should deliver lusty performance.

Upgraded brakes, wheels and tyres to match the 'go' of this MkIII.

test ride), then the most likely cause is the carburettors. The Amal Concentrics suit the Commando well, though the slides do wear after 10,000 miles or so. If wear isn't too bad, then new slides will be enough to cure it. A few bikes were converted to single SU or Mikuni carbs, which give good fuel figures. Misfiring is likely to be ignition trouble, especially if the bike still has points ignition – old, neglected plugs and HT leads are other possible culprits.

The clutch will feel heavy compared to that of a modern bike.

Clutch operation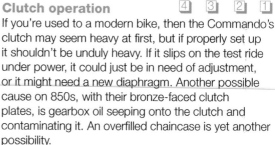

If you're used to a modern bike, then the Commando's clutch may seem heavy at first, but if properly set up it shouldn't be unduly heavy. If it slips on the test ride under power, it could just be in need of adjustment, or it might need a new diaphragm. Another possible cause on 850s, with their bronze-faced clutch plates, is gearbox oil seeping onto the clutch and contaminating it. An overfilled chaincase is yet another possibility.

If the clutch drags, then this should just be a matter of adjustment. If there's a rumbling noise when the clutch lever is pulled in, then the centre bearing is very worn.

Gears should engage cleanly and quietly.

Gearbox operation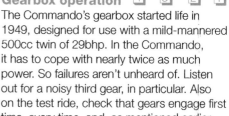

The Commando's gearbox started life in 1949, designed for use with a mild-mannered 500cc twin of 29bhp. In the Commando, it has to cope with nearly twice as much power. So failures aren't unheard of. Listen out for a noisy third gear, in particular. Also on the test ride, check that gears engage first time, every time, and, as mentioned earlier, play in the kickstart shaft indicates layshaft bearing wear.

Handling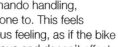

Much has been written and said over the years about Commando handling, in particular the high speed weave that all the bikes seem prone to. This feels unnerving at first, and one writer described it well as a nervous feeling, as if the bike is on tiptoes. The good news is that it isn't inherently dangerous and doesn't affect the bike's actual roadholding. Also, it only occurs at high speeds, so some riders may never experience it at all.

That apart, the Commando handles very well – any vagueness at lower speeds could be down to a number of factors, such as worn tyres, steering head bearings, shocks, forks and swing arm bearings, or out of adjustment isolastics.

Brakes

Don't expect modern stopping performance from the Commando's brakes. The front drum needs to be properly set up, while the Lockheed disc has a 'wooden' feel and isn't that powerful. That said, both brakes should haul the bike to a stop reasonably quickly.

A lightly rusted disc isn't a problem – peeling chrome is.

Early front discs were chromed – the plating could peel off, causing havoc with brake pad life, and the answer is to have the chrome skimmed off by an engineering shop, if this hasn't been done already. Disc calipers can seize if the bike isn't used for a long time (especially if it's put away after a wet winter ride) and MkIII calipers are particularly prone to this. Commando 750 calipers had no dust seals, so they need regular cleaning to stay effective – check that both pistons (inner and outer) move, though the inner is more prone to seizure. If the bike is stiff to push on the flat, then dragging discs are the most likely cause.

Calipers will seize if left unused for long periods.

As with many other aspects of the Commando, the brakes can be upgraded. A smaller-bore master cylinder is thought to improve the feel of the standard front disc, while a full twin-disc setup will give modern braking ability (at a price).

The front drum is powerful if properly set up.

Check out the rear drum on the test ride.

Cables

All the control cables – brakes, throttle and choke – should work smoothly, without stiffness or jerking. Poorly lubricated, badly

Cables should work smoothly.

adjusted cables are an indication of general neglect, and the same goes for badly routed cables.

Early horn/dipswitch.

Switchgear

Three types of switchgear were fitted to the Commando: the simple horn/dip control plus headlight switch for 1968-70; Lucas symmetrical alloy switches from 1971; and modern black switchgear on the final 850s. In all cases, check that the switches do what they're supposed to. Inconsistent operation is usually down to poor contacts within the switch itself, but new replacements are available.

Lucas alloy switch on later 750s/early 850s.

850 MkIII right-hand cluster.

Evaluation procedure
Add up the total points.
Score: 136 = excellent; 102 = good; 68 = average; 34 = poor.

Bikes scoring over 95 will be completely useable and will require only maintenance and care to preserve condition. Bikes scoring between 34 and 69 will require serious restoration (at much the same cost regardless of score). Bikes scoring between 70 and 94 will require very careful assessment of necessary repair/restoration costs in order to arrive at a realistic value.

10 Auctions
– sold! Another way to buy your dream

Auction pros & cons

Pros: Prices will usually be lower than those of dealers or private sellers, and you might grab a real bargain on the day. Auctioneers have usually established clear title with the seller. At the venue you can usually examine documentation relating to the bike.

Cons: You have to rely on a sketchy catalogue description of condition and history. The opportunity to inspect is limited, and you cannot ride the bike. Auction machines can be a little below par and may require some work. It's easy to overbid, and there will usually be a buyer's premium to pay in addition to the auction hammer price.

Which auction?

Auctions by established auctioneers are advertised in the motorcycle magazines and on the auction houses' websites. A catalogue, or a simple printed list of the lots for auction might be available only a day or two ahead, though often lots are listed and pictured on auctioneers' websites much earlier. Contact the auction company to ask if previous auction selling prices are available as this is useful information (details of past sales are often available on websites).

Catalogue, entry fee & payment details

When you purchase the catalogue of the bikes in the auction, it often acts as a ticket allowing two people to attend the viewing days and the auction. Catalogue details tend to be comparatively brief, but will include information such as 'one owner from new, low mileage, full service history', etc. It will also usually show a guide price to give you some idea of what to expect to pay, and will tell you what is charged as a buyer's premium. The catalogue will also contain details of acceptable forms of payment. At the fall of the hammer an immediate deposit is usually required, the balance payable within 24 hours. If you plan to pay by cash, note that there may be a cash limit. Some auctions will accept payment by debit card. Sometimes credit or charge cards are acceptable, but will often incur an extra charge. A bank draft or bank transfer will have to be arranged in advance with your own bank as well as with the auction house. No bike will be released before all payments are cleared. If delays occur in payment transfers then storage costs can accrue.

Buyer's premium

A buyer's premium will be added to the hammer price – don't forget this in your calculations. It is not usual for there to be a further state tax or local tax on the purchase price and/or on the buyer's premium.

Viewing

In some instances it's possible to view on the day, or days before, as well as in the hours prior to, the auction. There are auction officials available who are willing to help out if need be. While the officials may start the engine for you, a test ride is out of the question. Crawling under and around the bike as much as you want is permitted. You can also ask to see any available documentation.

Bidding

Before you take part in the auction, decide your maximum bid ... and stick to it! It may take a while for the auctioneer to reach the lot you're interested in, so use that time to observe how other bidders behave. When it's the turn of your bike, attract the auctioneer's attention and make an early bid. The auctioneer will then look to you for a reaction every time another bid is made. Usually the bids will be in fixed increments until the bidding slows, when smaller increments will often be accepted before the hammer falls. If you want to withdraw from the bidding, make sure the auctioneer understands your intentions – a vigorous shake of the head when he or she looks to you for the next bid should do the trick!

Assuming that you're the successful bidder, the auctioneer will note your card or paddle number, and from that moment on you will be responsible for the bike.

If it's unsold, either because it failed to reach the reserve or because there was little interest, it may be possible to negotiate with the owner, via the auctioneers, after the sale is over.

Successful bid

There are two more items to think about: how to get the bike home; and insurance. If you can't ride it, your own or a hired trailer is one way, another is to have it shipped using the facilities of a local company. The auction house will also have details of companies specialising in the transport of bikes.

Insurance for immediate cover can usually be purchased on site, but it may be more cost-effective to make arrangements with your own insurance company in advance, and then call to confirm the full details.

eBay & other online auctions?

eBay & other online auctions could land you a Commando at a bargain price, though you'd be foolhardy to bid without examining it first, something most vendors encourage. A useful feature of eBay is that the geographical location of the bike is shown, so you can narrow your choices to those within a realistic radius of home. Be prepared to be outbid in the last few moments of the auction. Remember, your bid is binding, and it will be very, very difficult to get restitution in the case of a crooked vendor fleecing you ... caveat emptor!

Be aware that some bikes offered for sale in online auctions are 'ghost' machines. Don't part with any cash without being sure that the vehicle does actually exist, and is as described (usually pre-bidding inspection is possible).

Auctioneers

See Chapter 16.

11 Paperwork
– correct documentation is essential!

The paper trail

Older bikes sometimes come with a portfolio of paperwork accumulated by previous owners. This documentation represents the real history of the machine, from which you can deduce how well it's been cared for, how much it's been used, which specialists have worked on it and major repairs and restoration dates. This information will be priceless to you as the new owner, so be wary of bikes with little paperwork supporting a claimed history.

Registration documents

All countries/states have some form of registration for private vehicles, such as the American 'pink slip' and the British 'log book' systems. It's essential to check that the registration document is genuine, that it relates to the vehicle in question, and that all details are correctly recorded, including frame and engine numbers (if these are shown). If buying from the previous owner, his or her name and address will be recorded in the document: this will not be the case if buying from a dealer.

In the UK the current (Euro-aligned) registration document is named 'V5C,' and is printed in coloured sections of blue, green and pink. The blue section relates to the bike's specification, the green section has details of the new owner, and the pink section is sent to the DVLA in the UK when the bike is sold. A small section in yellow deals with selling the bike within the motor trade.

Due to the introduction of important new legislation on data protection, it is no longer possible to acquire, from the DVLA, a list of previous owners of a bike you own, or are intending to purchase. This scenario will also apply to dealerships and other specialists you may wish to contact and acquire information on previous ownership and work carried out.

If the bike is an import, there may be expensive and time-consuming formalities to complete. Do you really want the hassle?

Roadworthiness certificate

Most country/state administrations require that vehicles are regularly tested to prove they are safe to use on the public highway and do not produce excessive emissions. In the UK that test (the 'MOT') is carried out at approved testing stations, for a fee. In the USA the requirement varies, but most states insist on an emissions test every two years as a minimum, while the police are charged with pulling over unsafe-looking vehicles.

In the UK the test is required on an annual basis once a vehicle becomes three years old. Of particular relevance for older bikes is that the certificate issued includes the mileage recorded at the test date and thus represents an independent record of that bike's history. Ask the seller if previous certificates are available. Without an MOT the vehicle should be trailered to its new home, unless you insist that a valid MOT is part of the deal. (Not such a bad idea this, as at least you'll know the bike was roadworthy on the day it was tested and you don't need to wait for the old certificate to expire before having the test done.)

In the UK, vehicles over 40 years old on May 20th each year, are exempt from MOT testing. Owners can still have the test carried out if they so wish.

Road licence

Every country/state charges some kind of tax for the use of its road system, the actual form of the 'road licence' and, how it is displayed, varying enormously.

Whatever the form, the road licence must relate to the vehicle carrying it and must be present and valid if the bike is to be driven on the public highway legally.

Changed legislation in the UK means that the seller of a motorcycle must surrender any existing road fund licence, and it is the responsibility of the new owner to re-tax the vehicle at the time of purchase and before the bike can be driven on the road. It's therefore vital to see the Vehicle Registration Certificate (V5C) at the time of purchase, and to have access to the New Keeper Supplement (V5C/2), allowing the buyer to obtain road tax immediately.

In the UK, vehicles 40 years old or more on the 1st January each year get free road tax. It's necessary to renew the tax status every year, even if there is no change.

If the bike is untaxed because it has not been used for a period of time, the owner has to inform the licensing authorities.

Certificates of authenticity

For many makes of older bike it is possible to get a certificate proving the age and authenticity (eg engine and frame numbers, paint colour and trim) of a particular machine. These are sometimes called 'Heritage Certificates' and if the bike comes with one of these it is a definite bonus. If you want to obtain one, the Norton Owners Club is the best starting point.

Valuation certificate

A recent valuation certificate, or letter signed by a recognised expert stating how much they believe the particular bike to be worth, are usually needed to get 'agreed value' insurance. This applies more to older classic bikes. In any case, such documents should act only as confirmation of your own assessment of the bike rather than a guarantee of value, as the expert may not have seen it in the flesh. The easiest way to find out how to obtain a formal valuation is via the Owners' Club.

Service history

These bikes may have been serviced at home by enthusiastic (and hopefully capable) owners for a good number of years. Nevertheless, try to obtain as much service history and other paperwork pertaining to the bike as you can. Naturally, specialist garage receipts score most points in the value stakes. Anything helps in the great authenticity game, items like the original bill of sale, handbook, parts invoices and repair bills, adding to the story and the character of the machine. Even a brochure correct to the year of the bike's manufacture is a useful document and something that you could well have to search hard to locate in future years.

If the seller claims to have carried out regular servicing, ask what work was completed, when, and seek some evidence of it being carried out. Your assessment of the bike's overall condition should tell you whether the seller's claims are genuine.

Restoration photographs

If the bike has been restored, expect to see receipts, and photographs taken while the work was under way. Pictures taken at various stages, and from various angles, should help you gauge the thoroughness of the work. If you buy the bike, ask for copies of all the photographs as they form an important part of its history.

12 What's it worth to you?

– let your head rule your heart!

Condition

If the bike you've been looking at is really ratty, then you've probably not bothered to use the marking system in Chapter 9 (30 minute evaluation). You may not have even got as far as using that chapter at all!

If you did use the marking system you'll know whether the bike is in Excellent (maybe concours), Good, Average or Poor condition or, perhaps, somewhere in between these categories.

To keep up-to-date with prices, buy the latest editions of the classic bike magazines and check the classified and dealer ads – these are particularly useful as they let you compare private and dealer prices. Most of the magazines run auction reports, which publish the actual selling prices, as do the auction houses' websites. Most of the dealers will have up-to-date websites as well.

Values have been fairly stable for some time, but some models will always be more sought-after than others. For example, it's clear that an original Production Racer will command a high price, but if you want an all-round practical classic, then that's not the bike for you. Prices can go down as well as up, but the Racer and the very early Plumstead-built Fastback will probably remain the most sought-after.

Bear in mind that a bike that is a recent show winner could be worth more than the highest price usually seen. Assuming that the bike you have in mind is not in show/concours condition, compare the level of condition that you judge it to be in with the appropriate price in the adverts. How does the figure compare with the asking price? Before you start haggling with the seller, consider what affect any variation from standard specification might have on the bike's value. This is a personal thing: for some, absolute originality is non-negotiable, while others see non-standard parts as an opportunity to pick up a bargain. Do your research in the reference books, so that you know the bike's spec when it left the factory. That way, you shouldn't end up paying a top-dollar price for a non-original bike.

If you're buying from a dealer, remember there will be a dealer's premium on the price.

Striking a deal

Negotiate on the basis of your condition assessment, mileage, and fault rectification cost. Also, take into account the bike's specification. Be realistic about the value, but don't be completely intractable: a small compromise on the part of the vendor or buyer will often facilitate a deal at little real extra cost.

13 Do you really want to restore?

– it'll take longer and cost more than you think ...

There's a romance about restoration projects, about bringing a sick bike back into blooming health, and it's tempting to buy something that 'just needs a few small jobs' to bring it up to scratch. But there are two things to think about: One, once you've got the bike home and start taking it apart, those few small jobs could turn into big ones. Two, restoration takes time, which is a precious thing in itself. Be honest with yourself – will you get as much pleasure from working on the bike as you will from riding it?

Of course, you could hand the whole lot over to a professional, and the biggest cost involved there is not the new parts, but the sheer labour involved. Such restorations don't come cheap, and, if taking this route, there are four other issues to bear in mind as well.

First, make it absolutely clear what you want doing. Do you want the bike to be 100 per cent original at the end of the process, or simply useable? Do you want a concours

Rebuilding an engine is a skilled job.

finish, or are you prepared to put up with a few blemishes on the original parts?

Second, make sure that not only is a detailed estimate involved, but that it is more or less binding. There have been instances where a person has been quoted one figure only to be presented with an invoice for a much larger one!

Third, check that the company

Just about all new parts, such as these crankcases, will be available.

you're dealing with has a good reputation – the owners club, or one of the reputable parts suppliers, should be able to make a few recommendations. Finally, having a Commando professionally restored may not make financial sense, as it may cost more than the finished bike will be worth. Not that this should put you off, if you have the budget, and really want to do it this way.

Ripe for restoration? There could be a perfectly good bike underneath.

Restoring a Commando requires a number of skills, which is fine if you already have them, but, if you haven't, it's good not to make your newly acquired bike part of the learning curve! Can you weld? Are you confident about building an engine? Do you have a warm, well-lit garage with a solid workbench and good selection of tools?

Be prepared for a top-notch professional to put you on a lengthy waiting list or, if tackling a restoration yourself, expect things to go wrong and set aside extra time to complete the task. Restorations can stretch into years when things like life intrude, so it's good to have some sort of target date.

A rolling restoration is tempting, especially as the summers start to pass with your bike still off the road. This is not the way to achieve a concours finish, which can only really be achieved via a thorough nut-and-bolt rebuild, without the bike getting

Attention to detail is key to a thorough restoration.

wet, gritty and salty in the meantime. But there's a lot to be said for a rolling restoration. Riding helps keep your interest up as the bike's condition improves, and it's also more affordable than trying to do everything in one go. In the long run, it will take longer, but you'll get some on-road fun out of the bike in the meantime.

14 Paint problems
– a bad complexion, including dimples, pimples and bubbles ...

Paint faults generally occur due to lack of protection/maintenance, or to poor preparation prior to a respray or touch-up. Some of the following conditions may be present in the bike you're looking at:

Orange peel
This appears as an uneven paint surface, similar to the appearance of the skin of an orange. The fault is caused by the failure of atomised paint droplets to flow into each other when they hit the surface. It's sometimes possible to rub out the effect with proprietary paint cutting/rubbing compound or very fine grades of abrasive paper. A respray may be necessary in severe cases. Consult a paint shop for advice.

Cracking
Severe cases are likely to have been caused by too heavy an application of paint (or filler beneath the paint). Also, insufficient stirring of the paint before application can lead to the components being improperly mixed, and cracking can result. Incompatibility with the paint already on the panel can have a similar effect. To rectify, it's necessary to rub down to a smooth, sound finish before respraying the problem area.

Crazing
Sometimes the paint takes on a crazed rather than a cracked appearance when the problems mentioned under 'cracking' are present. This problem can also be caused by a reaction between the underlying surface and the paint. Removing the paint and respraying the problem area is usually the only solution.

Crazing has a number of causes.

Blistering
Almost always caused by corrosion of the metal beneath the paint. Usually the metal will be found to be perforated, and the damage will usually be worse than that suggested by the area of blistering. The metal will have to be repaired before repainting.

Micro blistering
Usually the result of an economy respray, where inadequate heating has allowed moisture to settle on the surface before spraying. Consult a paint specialist, but damaged paint will have to be removed before partial or full respraying. Can also be caused by bike covers that don't 'breathe.'

Fading

Some colours, especially reds, are prone to fading if subject to strong sunlight for long periods without the benefit of polish protection. Sometimes proprietary paint restorers and/or paint cutting/rubbing compounds will retrieve the situation. Often a respray is the only real solution.

Faded but otherwise good original paint on this 850.

Peeling

Often a problem with metallic paintwork when the sealing lacquer becomes damaged and begins to peel off. Poorly applied paint may also peel. The remedy is to strip and start again.

Dimples

Dimples in the paintwork are caused by the residue of polish (particularly silicone types) not being removed properly before respraying. Paint removal and repainting is the only solution.

Pinstripes wear away with time.

A good respray in original colours can look fantastic.

15 Problems due to lack of use

– just like their owners, Commandos need exercise!

Like any piece of engineering, and indeed like human beings, Nortons deteriorate if they sit doing nothing for long periods. This is especially relevant if the bike is laid up for six months of the year, as some classic bikes are.

Rust

If the bike is put away wet, and/ or stored in a cold, damp garage, the paint, metal and brightwork will suffer. Ensure the machine is completely dry and clean before going into storage, and, if you can afford it, invest in a dehumidifier to keep the garage atmosphere dry.

Damp causes rust.

Seized components

Pistons in brake calipers can seize partially or fully, giving binding or non-working brakes. Cables are also vulnerable to seizure – the solution being to thoroughly lube them before storage, and giving them a couple of pulls once a week or so.

Tyres

If the bike's been left on its side stand, most of its weight is on the tyres, and flat spots and cracks will develop over time. Always leave the bike on its centre stand, as this takes the weight off the tyres.

Engine

Old, acidic oil can corrode bearings. Many riders change the oil in the spring, when they're putting the bike back on the road, but really it should be changed just before the bike is laid up, so that the bearings are sitting in fresh oil. The same goes for the gearbox. While you're giving the cables their weekly exercise, turn the engine over

Brake calipers will begin to seize.

slowly on the kickstart, ignition off. Don't start it though – running the engine for a short time does more harm than good, as it produces a lot of moisture internally, which the engine doesn't get hot enough to burn off. That will attack the engine internals, and the silencers. Beware of the engine wet sumping over time, and, on 850 MkIIIs, that the primary chain tensioner may lose its oil.

Battery/electrics
Either remove the battery and give it a top-up charge every couple of weeks, or connect it to a battery top-up device, such as the Optimate, which will keep it permanently fully charged. Damp conditions will allow fuses and earth connections to corrode, storing electrical troubles for the spring. Eventually, wiring insulation will harden and fail.

Tyres deteriorate over time, especially if carrying weight.

16 The Community

– key people, organisations and companies in the Commando world

Auctioneers

Bonhams www.bonhams.com
British Car Auctions (BCA) www.bca-europe.com or www.british-car-auctions.co.uk
Cheffins www.cheffins.co.uk
Dorset Vintage & Classic Auctions www.dvca.co.uk
eBay www.ebay.com
H&H www.classic-auctions.co.uk
Shannons www.shannons.com.au
Silver www.silverauctions.com

Clubs across the world

Norton Owners Club – UK
www.nortonownersclub.org

International Norton Owners Association – USA
www.inoanorton.com

Norton Owners Club of Victoria – Australia
www.victoria.nortonownersclub.org

Norton Owners Club of NSW – Australia
www.nocnsw.org.au

Norton Owners Club – New Zealand
www.nocnz.org.nz

Norton Owners Club – France
www.norton-club-fr.org

Norton Owners Club – Denmark
www.nortons.dk

Norton Owners Club – Netherlands
www.nortonclubnederland.nl

Norton Commando forum
www.accessnorton.com

Join the club!

Specialists

There are many specialists supplying Commando spare parts, and to list them all
would take up more space than we have here, so we've restricted this list to UK

suppliers – those at the top of the list specialise in Norton or Commando parts only, the ones further down the list deal in British bike spares more generally, including the Commando.

Norton only

Norvil Motorcycle Company – spares, special parts, new bikes.
www.norvilmotorcycle.co.uk Tel: 01543 278008

Andover Norton International – spares.
www.andover-norton.co.uk Tel: 01488 686816

Mick Hemmings Motorcycles – spares, special parts.
www.mickhemmings.co.uk Tel: 01604 638505

RGM Motors – spares, Cumbria.
www.rgmmotors.co.uk Tel: 01946 841517

Middleton Engineering – Commando performance parts.
www.stevemaney.com Tel: 01924 265158

Norman White (Norton) – special parts, new Production Racer.
www.normanwhite.co.uk Tel: 01264 773326

British bike spares/restorations

A Gagg & Sons – spares, Nottingham.
www.gagg-and-sons.freeserve.co.uk Tel: 0115 978 6288

Britbits – spares, Bournemouth.
www.britbits.co.uk Tel: 01202 483675

Burton Bike Bits – spares, Staffs.
www.burtonbikebits.net Tel: 01530 564362

Carl Rosner – spares, London.
www.carlrosner.co.uk Tel: 020 8657 0121

High Gear Engine Centre – engine work.
Tel: 020 8942 2828

Richard Hacker – spares, London.
Tel: 020 8659 4045

Robin James Engineering – restorations.
www.robinjamesengineering.com Tel: 01568 612800

Russell Motors – spares, London.
www.russellmotors.co.uk Tel: 020 7228 1714

SRM Engineering – spares, rebuilds.
www.srm-engineering.com Tel: 01970 627771

Books

British Motorcycles Since 1950, Vol 3
Steve Wilson, PSL, 1992

Norton Commando
Mick Duckworth, Haynes, 2004

Norton Commando: Ultimate Portfolio
RM Clarke (ed), Brooklands Books, 2001

Norton: The Complete History
Derek Magrath, Crowood, 1997

Commando Service Notes
Tim Stevens & John Hudson, Norton Owners Club, 1979

17 Vital statistics
– essential data at your fingertips

Listing the vital statistics of every Commando variant would take far more room than we have here, so we've picked three representative models:

Max speed
1968 Commando	122mph
1972 Roadster 750	110mph
1977 Interstate 850	111mph

Engine
1968 Commando	Air-cooled parallel twin, 745cc. Bore and stroke 73 x 89mm. Compression ratio 8.9:1. 58bhp @ 6500rpm
1972 Roadster 750	Air-cooled parallel twin, 745cc. Bore x stroke 73 x 89mm. Compression ratio 10.1:1. 65bhp @ 6800rpm
1977 Interstate 850	Air-cooled parallel twin, 828cc. Bore x stroke 77 x 89mm. Compression ratio 7.7:1. 58bhp @ 5900rpm

Gearbox
1968 Commando	Four-speed. Ratios: 1st 12.40:1, 2nd 8.25:1, 3rd 5.9:1, 4th 4.84:1.
1972 Roadster 750	Four-speed. Ratios: 1st 12.40:1, 2nd 8.25:1, 3rd 5.9:1, 4th 4.84:1.
1977 Interstate 850	Four-speed. Ratios: 1st 11.79:1, 2nd 7.83:1, 3rd 5.57:1, 4th 4.60:1

Brakes
1968 Commando	Cable, 8in front twin-leading shoe drum, 8in rear drum
1972 Roadster 750	Front hydraulic disc 10.7in, rear cable drum 7in
1977 Interstate 860	Hydraulic 10.7in discs front and rear

Electrics
1968 Commando	12-volt, alternator
1972 Roadster 750	12-volt, alternator
1977 Interstate 850	12-volt, alternator

Weight
1968 Commando	415lb
1972 Roadster 750	395lb (dry)
1977 Interstate 850	492lb

Major change points by model years
1968: Commando enters production.

1969: S type, R type, and Interpol launched. MkII with points in timing cover, external rpm drive, twin 6-volt coils.

1970: Roadster and Production Racer launched, frame strengthened.

1971: SS type, Hi-Rider and Fastback LR launched. MkIII with naked forks, 4.10 tyres, centre stand mounting on engine plates, Lucas switchgear.

1972: Interstate launched. Combat engine, 32mm carbs, front disc brake, stronger crankcases, new prop stand. Later in year, Superblend main bearings, revised head gasket, lower compression. Sintered bronze faced clutch plates.

1973: Commando 850 launched as Roadster, Interstate, Hi-Rider and Interpol. Square rear light, black instrument cases, stronger centre stand and head steady, improved valves, chain guard extension, Lucas 10CA auto-advance, front disc standard on all but Hi-Rider. Late in year MkIIA with black cap silencers, big plastic airbox, higher second gear.

1974: John Player Special launched. Left-hand disc brake, improved exhaust downpipe mounting, instruments with squiggly 'NVT' logo.

1975: 850 MkIII with electric start, left-foot gearchange, front and rear disc brakes, hydraulic primary chain tensioner, anti-drain valve in timing cover, vernier adjustment for isolastics, high-output Lucas RM24 alternator. Late in year, production ceases, workers' sit-in aims to restart with updated Commando.

1976: Sit-in ends, batch of 500 Commandos built.

1977: Final main batch of 1500 Commandos built.

1978: Small number of Commandos built up from spares.

Engine numbers

126125	1968	I	750	Commando, engine prefix 20M3
131180	1969	I	750	Now called Fastback, engine prefix 20M3
131257	1969	II	750	S, SS, R type, engine prefix 20M3S
135140	1970	II	750	First Roadster (low pipes, upswept silencers)
141783	1971	III	750	Fastback, Roadster, SS, Hi-Rider, Fastback Long Range
200000	1972	IV	750	Hi-Rider, Interstate
220000	1973	V	750	Roadster, Hi-Rider, Interstate
300000	1973	I	850	Hi-Rider, Interstate
306591	1973	IA	850	Roadster, Interstate
307311	1974	II/IIA	850	Roadster, Hi-Rider, Interstate
325001	1975	III	850	Roadster, Hi-Rider, Interstate

Also from Veloce Publishing –

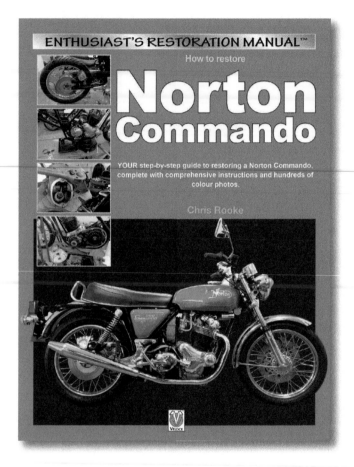

Written in a friendly and accessible manner by an enthusiast of many years, this book provides a thorough and detailed restoration guide for the Norton Commando, complete with step-by-step instructions, and hundreds of colour photos.

ISBN: 978-1-787113-94-7
Paperback • 27x20.7cm • 224 pages • 820 pictures

www.velocebooks.com / www.veloce.co.uk
All current books • New book news • Special offers • Gift vouchers • Forum

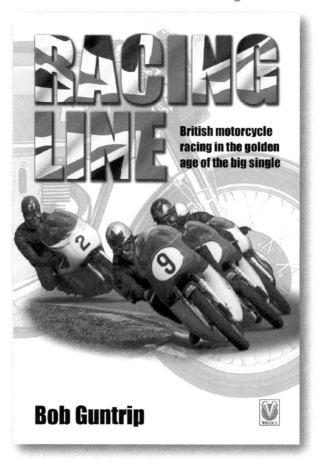

British motorcycle racing in the golden age of the big single

Bob Guntrip

Racing Line is the story of big-bike racing in Britain during the 1960s –
when the British racing single reached its peak; when exciting racing
unfolded at circuits across the land every summer; and when Britain took
its last great generation of riding talent and engineering skill to the world.

ISBN: 978-1-845847-93-7
Hardback • 22.5x15.2cm • 232 pages • 76 colour and b&w pictures

Index